Aaron Hedges

A Case Study
in the Rapture and the
End of Life as We Know It

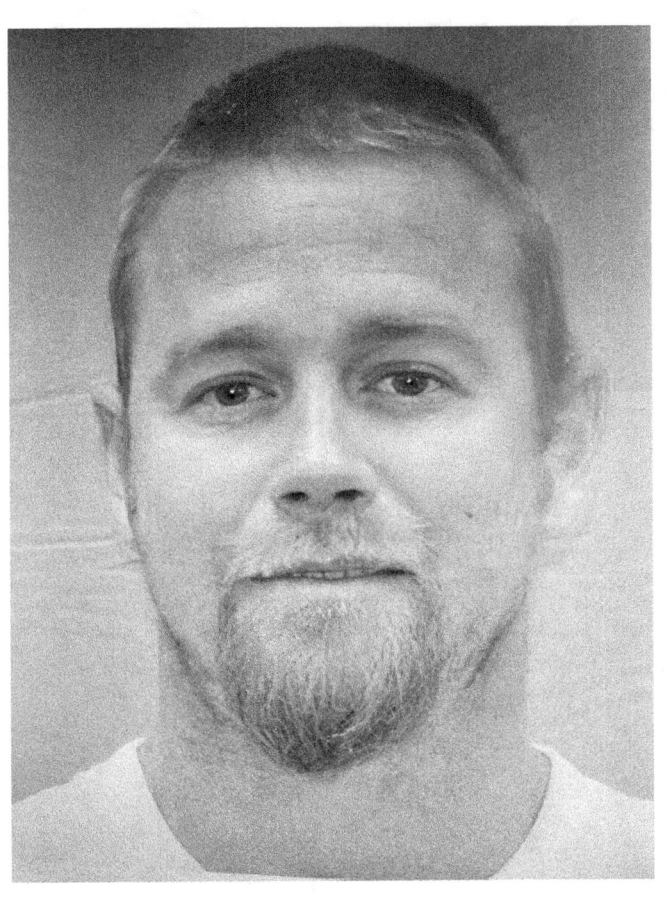

To request permission, contact the author at:
ameliahathow@gmail.com

ISBN: 978-1-958150-90-0
Aaron Hedges: A Case Study of the Rapture and the End of Life as We Know It

Paperback edition, April 2022

SUBJECTS
BODY, MIND & SPIRIT / Channeling & Mediumship
BODY, MIND & SPIRIT / Unexplained Phenomena
PHILOSOPHY / Metaphysics

Aaron Hedges

A Case Study
in the Rapture and the End of
Life as We Know It

by

Amelia Hathow

TABLE OF CONTENTS

INTRODUCTION

Sometimes it is from the least expected places that understanding occurs.

This book was created for you to reflect on the story of a skilled hunter who mysteriously went missing in the mountains. The reflection on his story is presented for you to consider the implications of not having control of what happens around us, what happens to us, and even how we act ourselves. This book is meant for you to consider that sometimes outside influences affect our actions, our perceptions, and the outcomes of both.

This book presents channeled messages (hand written by a psychic medium, and also typed out in case you cannot make out the written words) that are within this book interpreted in the lens of understanding the Rapture as told in the Bible.

It is especially timely now as so many people, in our Covid affected society, are wondering when the Rapture will occur as there seems to be a collective feeling that the end is near.

As you read this account, please consider that anything is possible. The most important thing is to be aware and to pay attention. Not just to what you are trying to accomplish, but to what is happening around you and to notice things you do sometimes may feel like you aren't in control of them, such as when you are acting out of character.

Though you are responsible for your actions and the outcome of your actions, know that sometimes your actions are influenced by outside sources. Knowing this might help you not only understand what is happening in your own life, but understand why other people, especially the people you love, sometimes act in ways that go against what you think they would do.

Aaron's Story

Aaron Hedges, along with a couple of friends, set out on September 3, 2014, to hunt for elk in a mountain range called the "Crazies," located in central Montana. After two days of hiking together, on September 5, Aaron went off on his own to a location at Sunlight Lake, to a site where one of his friends had stored away camping equipment on an earlier hike. Aaron's friends didn't hear from him for a few hours, so they called him; he didn't answer, but they could see his GPS coordinates through the communication devices they shared and noticed that he had taken a wrong turn and was further away than he should have been.

Elk hunting can be a solo sport, which was the case for Aaron especially being familiar with the terrain he was in. So, it isn't unusual that his friends waited a day before they went looking for him. All this happened as a huge storm moved in and dumped two feet of snow on the mountain range. After two days passed, Aaron was reported missing to the county sheriff department. Park County and Sweet Grass County began an extensive search involving multiple animal and human rescue teams.

On September 9, 2014, Aaron's boots and a few other belongings were found by a dog rescue team. Some found it odd that his boots were neatly placed side by side, which was interpreted to mean there was no distress in him going missing. Some of the searchers, who have a lot of experience, noted it was very odd that they had not seen the boots at that particular location when they had been in the same spot a day or two before. There was speculation that Aaron may have had hypothermia, as they considered it odd behavior that Aaron seemed to have left his boots behind in such rough terrain.

Officially the search for Aaron Hedges ended on September 22, 2014. Nine months later, on June 22, 2015, someone found additional items that belonged to Aaron Hedges, including his hunting vest, backpack, license, and hunting bow. It was noticed that his backpack was purposefully placed against a tree and not far from a nearby home. On August 8, 2016, Aaron's skull, pelvis, a femur, cell phone, and a thin jacket were found.

David Paulides, an investigative author who has written numerous books titled Missing 411, was interested in Aaron Hedges's case and wondered what caused Aaron to go so drastically off course. Paulides also wondered how a person, with possible hypothermia and no boots on, could walk in a foot or two of snow, with his backpack, bow, and other items six miles away from where he left his boots.

There are many questions about how and why Aaron went missing and how he died. This book may shed some light on those unsolved mysteries.

GUIDANCE FROM RELIGIOUS TEXTS

We are born and we die. This much is certain. Hopefully in between we live our life as righteously (as correctly) as possible. So that we can do the best we can, have little judgment of others, and work to fulfill our own God-given purpose. There is a lot of speculation as to what happens after life, which could result in having fear about death. For some people the fear is in the uncertainty of what the afterlife looks like. For others it is about the unknown pain that might accompany the dying process. Do we meet up with loved ones who have already passed? Do we meet God or are we sent back to earth to try again?

The concept of the Rapture is relatively new to Christianity, and has been noted to have been brought to prominence by Evangelical Protestant theologians to discuss the "mystical union with God for eternal life in Heaven." In essence, the Rapture is a good thing, but as it is associated with an end-time event where "all Christian believers who are alive, along with resurrected believers, would rise 'in the clouds, to meet the Lord in the air,'" it is also seen as slightly negative. [Wikipedia] This negative perception comes mainly from the notion that it will come at an unexpected time, and from an influence seen as outside of ourselves.

There are three passages from the Bible that are relevant to the concept of the Rapture that this book aims to bring awareness to:

- 1 Thessalonians 4:13–18
- 1 Corinthians 15:50-52
- Matthew 24

In Thessalonians, Paul the Apostle uses the Greek verb arapazo, which means "to snatch" or "to seize," when he "explains that believers in Jesus Christ would be snatched away from the earth into the air." At the end of life, the end of time, "the Lord Himself will descend from heaven with a shout, with the voice of an archangel, and with the trumpet of God. And the dead in Christ will rise first." [16]

Whether we are sleeping or paying attention makes no difference. If we believe in Christ, then God will take us. We are to be comforted by this notion. Being snatched is a GOOD thing – even if it sounds more like an abduction. What is important to come to terms with and implement in our lives is to live each day, each moment, to the best of our ability. If we contemplate on a daily basis and live a faith-filled life, then when the end comes, we are most likely to be in a position to have no doubt that we will go to God, if that is our belief. The Thessalonians passage encourages us to have no doubt that God will take us safely into his care.

In the Corinthians passage, we read that "in a flash, in the twinkling of an eye, at the last trumpet. For the trumpet will sound, the dead will be raised imperishable, and we will be changed." [52]

This can be a literal end or a figurative end. In the Rapture, it is literal. We will be changed from living to dead, even if that means being with God. But even if you don't believe in the biblical notion, you can see that there is a change.

The Matthew 24 verse is quite long, but much easier to understand. It states that two men will be in a field, and one will be taken up. What does this mean? It means that for every two people, only one lives his/her life as a "good" Christian. A true believer. This is powerful. Only half of us are living how we are supposed to live. Even if you aren't a Christian, this is true. If you are not honest, if you do not treat others as you want to be treated, you are not a chosen one. In fact, this might even mean that you will never end your eternal suffering. And that this "snatching up" could be a real thing and could have been happening to others for quite some time now.

My understanding of these passages as they relate to the Rapture is that it is important that we take responsibility for our actions, and that we are thoughtful in how we live our lives. When we are driven by greed, competition, and/or selfishness, we are not living a pure life.

Following the message of the Bible and worshiping Christ sometimes brings excessive judgment of others as we feel we know best when it comes to how to live life properly. This is ironic because Jesus is said to have taught unconditional love and acceptance of others regardless of who they are and how they identify. The Bible teaches us that God has the final judgment; it is not the responsibility or job of humans to take on this type of role.

The Hindu story, the Bhagavad Gita, states that it is better to live your own destiny imperfectly than another's destiny perfectly. [BG 18.47] Sometimes we think we can do something better than someone else. That might be true. But what are we here on this planet to do? We are here to fulfill our OWN purpose, not someone else's.

However, what if being snatched in the Rapture was in fact a punishment? What if we are mistaken in just how Christian we are? What if we are not actually following Christ even though we are a believer?

We might wonder why things happen to certain people. Why are we presented with particular life struggles? Evangelical Protestantism suggests that the Rapture will unite Jesus followers with God. But what if the perception of a Jesus follower is the opposite of their action? What if those who are positioning themselves as just, righteous, are actually not good neighbors?

This reminds me of the Tower of Babel – the idea was that the builders of this tower wanted to reach the heavens. It is noted in Genesis that it was like a competition between God and humans. The tyrant Nimrod ordered the people to build a tower to get them closer to God. At that time civilization was being created and people were working together. It seemed for the common good, but it was also a matter of hubris, a defiance against God, as they acted as if they knew better than God. They set aside the design of how hierarchy works, from the top down, not from the ground up. A good example of "Babel" is allowing one's children to run the household (an increasingly present situation these days). God's punishment was to topple the tower, creating a division amongst the people in that they were not able to communicate as they each had a different language. How interesting that our differences as humans would come primarily in the form of language, in our inability to communicate? Language seems to inform culture, and though we currently use race to divide us, race came from culture, which came from language.

With this in mind, it is important that we understand that the Rapture gives people a false sense of righteousness. Most accounts of the Rapture put believers as those who are going straight to heaven. But rather than leaving behind a period of political chaos and personal torment, what if the Rapture took those who are causing this torment? What if the Rapture took away those who are not good keepers of the earth? What if the Rapture took the "bad" and left the "good"? What if failing to take care of the earth and caring for other people, despite our religious ideology, put us into the "bad" category?

The last two years (Covid-19) have taught us that we must prepare for the end of times, regardless of how it happens, regardless of who we think is good and who is bad. What if Covid-19 was put on Earth as the current Tower of Babel? What if too many righteous people inflicting judgment actually caused Covid-19 to be unleashed on us to break down our hubris?

Is it possible for us to have redemption?

How It All Works

After I retired from my busy classroom of constant chatter of mostly 6-7 year olds, I learned to quiet my mind and began to hear a guiding voice that came from within, or so I thought. The voice was very faint and I could feel it more than I could hear it. This began my curiosity about what I was experiencing. With more time on my hands I started to explore how this was possible, feeling someone else's words rather than hearing them. I began to read different materials that might explain what I was experiencing including the Mahabharata, the Torah, the Khabala, the chakra system, science books, and books on mediumship. I also began to consult with local mediums for insight and a direction to take with this new found discovery. Practicing different types of mediumship was also crucial for me to understand the many possibilities and to begin to understand what I was best at. Even though, as a child, I had experiences sensing people who had passed, my experiences at this point were more prominent.

My knowing, from some 50 years earlier, started to become a reality. I began to sense that there were particular entities who wanted to talk to (through) me. This understanding didn't happen overnight. I practiced, continued to talk with others, and realized that I was tapping into something greater than myself. However, I discovered something that enhances mediumship abilities: personal development. I was working on my personal issues at the same time as I was practicing mediumship. I found out that since everything is God's, we own nothing. Even when we express ourselves in any way, we are only expressing what God has created for us beforehand, even emotions, thoughts, and ideas. This means that there is nothing new. Because of this we are all mediums at physical birth and beyond physical body perishment. There are different degrees of mediums as there are different degrees of temperature. Personal development changes the degree of one's mediumship. I began learning and practicing several things; seeing beyond myself, reducing my fears about life and death, experiencing different types of nothingness, emotionally detaching from everything, learning to let my mind go blank, and much more. In turn, this reduced the amount of distractions I had in order for me to feel and see the more subtle areas of our reality where communication with others who are not in a more dense version of themselves (physical body) is possible.

My best mediumship skill is channel writing. I also eventually learned that the initial guiding voice I thought came from within actually came from outside of myself. It wasn't me at all. It was someone or something trying to talk to me, though at that time I had too many distractions to be able to "hear" clearly. As I reduced the distractions I had, what was being relayed to me became very clear. Most of the messages I was getting and writing down were about life lessons they had learned from the life they had lived that they wanted to pass along in order for us to live a more fulfilled life.

During an evening of binging Netflix programs, particularly Missing 411... I sensed Aaron Hedges' presence and understood he wanted to share his story along with the Entity that took him. That was in July 2020. Aaron and the Entity that took him periodically requested that I record their messages through January 2021. It took a full 13 months of taking down other messages and processing information for something basic to dawn on me: Aaron Hedges' story, the way he was telling it to me, was in essence how the Rapture works.

Last week I sat down and took a message titled "The Rapture." That's when I made the connection between the messages that had come from the year before. Sometimes we need time to understand things that in hindsight appear to be obvious.

In this book, all of the relevant messages I received are shared. There are two "sides" to the story... The other side of this story is the Entity that apparently was the one who "abducted" Aaron. This Entity gives us some other possibilities about life to think about. Pay close attention to what and how they are relaying their messages. The structural content is important as well. Everything matters.

I will attempt in this little book to share with you the connections between Aaron, the entity, and the Rapture. I believe there is an important point for us to understand as we await the Rapture that is being talked about so much lately, especially with Covid-19, political strife, and an escalating number of other disturbing events, all of which are fueled by fear and reduce the chance of true solidarity amongst us all. Hope still remains, but is slowly fading away to its despair.

The underlying message is to be aware of your own participation in life, so that you might avoid being the one taken in the Rapture, unless perhaps you are ready to reunite with your loved ones, with God, or perhaps be sent back to try again.

REFLECTION ON THE MESSAGES

The end of the world comes with many interpretations. The end times, the Rapture, and now, in Spring 2022, we are asked to focus on a possible beginning of World War III. There is a lot of confusion, and as a society we are largely looking outside of ourselves (to news and others who we believe have our best interests in mind) for answers and clarity.

It is time for you to understand for yourself what is going on. And to consider how different influences have an effect on not only what you see, but also what you do.

What if.... Aaron was guided to take his shoes off? What if he felt a vibration that made him do things he wouldn't normally do? My impression is that Aaron went from a usually low, negative vibration to a higher, more positive one, influenced by an outside source, which propelled him to take his boots off and proceed in ways that seem unusual. The people who searched for him after he went missing speculated that hypothermia may have caused Aaron's confusion. What if he was influenced by a different source?

The first message I took from Aaron, on July 5, 2020, notes that Aaron was "shivering" – this could imply he was cold, but it could also have been a sensation in his body he wasn't familiar with – a vibration that compelled him to go in a direction other than what he had said he would go.

The second message, which I took down on the same day as the first, Aaron says that "My body began vibrating at a different level." He was mesmerized by it. He wanted to understand it. My interpretation now is that there was a force outside of himself that influenced him to act in an unusual way.

That same day, I recorded a message that appeared to me as "above" Aaron. I wasn't sure who or what this entity was. It was clear that this one Entity was representing a larger collective. The main idea of that message was that humans put unequal weight on the life of a human over other life forms. To me this is an interesting concept, and one that I hadn't considered before. It is absolutely true. We see building greater and larger buildings as a good thing. What if our ego and greed is causing the destruction of the planet? What if our insensitivity to oneself and one another is the very cause of the Rapture?

A few days later, I received another message from Aaron. It points to the importance of working daily to fulfill your purpose in life. I noted this in relation to the Hindu text in an earlier chapter. Society takes us away from our true purpose. We are pushed and encouraged to get a better job, make more money, and buy more objects (the production of which actually aids in the destruction of our natural environment). The bigger the house, the more important the man. What if the bigger the heart was all that mattered? What if we could all be "small," without having to have any importance?

What if money wasn't how we are known, but by our actions that are driven by our heart?

The response from the Entity was to take your time. Now I interpret this as having to do with meditation and other ways of remaining silent. Usually when we are rushing from one accomplishment to the next, we fail to listen to ourselves, to be motivated by our true purpose. We get in the habit of being busy, when what would be so beneficial would be to be still, to be quiet, for a little longer.

A week later I received two messages from the Entity. This is when I started to sense this was someone not quite the same as us. Due to the mention of magnetism and non-human interactions, I did a little research as they asked. Though I didn't take proper notes, I remember thinking that within the human body some atoms hold a magnetic charge, and that a huge magnet outside of ourselves would have the ability to cause a vibration in our body – one that would not be explainable as a "normal" body sensation. The message from July 14, 2020, stated that "magnetism also works with thoughts" – this phrase is what keeps me thinking that sometimes our actions are the result of an influence outside of ourselves. It is hard to believe, hard to accept, this concept, but I urge you to think about it. Meditate or contemplate on it.

Are all your thoughts coming from your own self? A message from the Entity on July 18, 2020, encourages us to slow down, to reflect, to just be. "Clear your mind even further" - let go of the ideas you think you are supposed to have. Find your own truth.

Almost six weeks passed before I received another message from Aaron (August 28). Looking back at it now, it is a reiteration, though in more specifics, of what the Entity had last said. Pay very close attention to words that appear in your daily life in a recurring way. It is as if there is a coded message, and if we pay attention to it, we will understand our true purpose in life. We are encouraged again to slow down and be truly aware of our reality.

It was another six weeks before Aaron came back with an important message (October 9). He tells us we are one with the earth – that we not only leave behind our trash, but also our tears, our love, our beauty. He seems to implore us to be better keepers of our earth, because it is our energy that decomposes into the earth. He encourages us to be more positive, to find happiness.

In November Aaron came with two messages. Both of them have to do with joy and love. The first was about balancing a feeling of bliss with an awareness of your environment. In the second Aaron indicated that he felt a surge inside himself, a shock of love. He called it near euphoria. Though he went missing, he indicated to me that he felt true, pure love. He wants us to be paying attention to such flashes in our lives so that we become familiar with them to such a degree that they don't shock you into your heart stopping.

The last message from Aaron came more than three months later, on January 23, 2021 – six and a half months from the first message. The previous two messages were tied to pure love, to acceptance, whereas this January message, along with his general advice to pay attention, seems to question what you will do when the Rapture comes. Will you give up, or will you try to hold on to your life? I see holding on to the tree as a metaphor for being a good keeper of the earth. Of living a righteous life, one free of greed, one full of good deeds, one filled with love, understanding, and compassion.

More than a year passed from that last message from Aaron when I had an understanding that appeared from outside of myself, that connected the Rapture with Aaron. On February 21, 2022, I took down the message entitled "The Rapture" that features a horseshoe as a metaphor for how we are meant to serve. How we are here on this earth for a specific purpose, something greater than we can actually understand. When we attempt to accomplish that which is not our purpose, we are going against our true nature. We have a certain responsibility in being aware of what our purpose is.

There are other forces at work as well. I will go back to the bible now, as that is how/where the Rapture is introduced to us. In my experience there are many (certainly not all) people who do not act in a Christian way. Meaning they go against the 10 Commandments – they kill, they steal, they commit adultery, they do not honor their mother and father, they do not love their neighbor as themselves, etc. I also know people who judge others, who say "he's going to hell" – as if they are the deciding factor. What I've learned from these conversations is that not all people have the same level of faith. Some act righteously. Others unjustly.

What the messages that are included in this book have shown me is that we may have the idea of Rapture wrong. Before these messages came to me, I assumed that the Rapture meant everyone dies. But now I believe that those who are not good keepers of our earth are the ones who will perish.

Those who blindly follow Christ may suffer the most because they put too much stock into what they have been taught about Christ being their savior, for forgiving all sins, without a true understanding of the repercussions of the actions from daily life activities. In reality, each of those sins (decisions) must be returned with an equal and opposite reaction. It is not someone else's responsibility to bail us out or to change what we deserve. We take on full responsibility for our actions. We must understand that we are our own savior.

So we have a chance to make things "right" – we can change the way we behave, our belief system in total, actually. So is it a matter of will you cling on to that tree for dear life in the face of a tsunami? Are you ready for death as just another experience, as you trust that the result of it will leave you exactly where you are meant to be?

What do you focus on? Is it coming from within or are you being asked to proselytize that which you don't really know?

My sincere hope is that you will thoughtfully consider the messages in this book, and that you will reflect on your own life and actions, and that you will be aware of the possibility that there are forces at work outside of yourself that affect your own behavior. It is all very heavy, and certainly complicated. But all worth considering. Try turning off the TV sometimes and instead of passing time, to wonder and think instead.

It will impact the earth, our society, your life.

There is no need to be worried or scared about the Rapture if you are a good person, who is actively working to fulfill your purpose in life. Even with outside influences, you have the ability to keep working towards good.

THE MESSAGES

2-21-22   The Rapture

Horses wear shoes that are nailed to their feet. Like thorses' shoes we are all connected. We are tacked on, willing or not. In service or in slavery. Is there a choice? That's not the point. The point is what you do with where you are. Are you a victim only? Or do you make the situation (for the horse) better? See yourself as a support and you will be more sturdy. You provide the stability and comfort the horse needs to do its job better. When you cry and complain you are prone to make it stumble and potentially fall. And you know that when a horse breaks its leg it must be shot. Accept that as a horseshoe that you have great potential to help a greater good. To help a much larger mission than you may even be able to comprehend. Serve your purpose without complaint. Trust there is a reason for your participation. Do not waste time trying to identify it or reason (weasle) out of it. If a rock is put in front of you, either move it or go around. Don't keep looking at it and wondering why it is there. That's not the point. Just get past it. Know that as a horse shoe that you are serving a purpose that is greater than you. Take pride in that awareness. Your purpose is not to be a fence or a door handle or anything else. It is to be a shoe for a horse.

Impression — This msg is for those who are trying to change themselves into what they shouldn't be — they do not have true faith in their life's purpose. Don't change — you are perfect just the way you are.

2-21-22

The Rapture

Horses wear shoes that are nailed to their feet. Like horses' shoes we are all connected. We are tacked on, willing or not. In service or in slavery. Is there a choice? That's not the point. The point is what you do with where you are. Are you a victim only? Or do you make the situation (for the horse) better? See yourself as a support and you will be more sturdy. You provide the stability and comfort the horse needs to do its job better. When you cry and complain you are prone to make it stumble and potentially fall. And you know that when a horse breaks its leg it must be shot. Accept that as a horseshoe that you have great potential to help a greater good. To help a much larger mission than you may even be able to comprehend. Serve your purpose without complaint. Trust there is a reason for your participation. Do not waste time trying to identify it or reason (weasel) out of it. If a rock is put in front of you, either move it or go around it. Don't keep looking at it and wondering why it is there. That's not the point. Just get past it. Know that as a horseshoe that you are serving a purpose that is greater than you. Take pride in that awareness. Your purpose is not to be a fence or a door handle or anything else. It is to be a shoe for a horse.

Impression:

This message is for those who are trying to change themselves into what they shouldn't be - they do not have <u>true</u> faith in their life's purpose. Don't change - you are perfect just the way you are.

7-5.20 Aaron Hedges

Dieing alone is scary. Especially when you don't know what happen. I was pulled right up from the ground. I didnt feel anyone or see anyone. I was just floating upward. Then I Blacked out Or at least I have no other memory until I passed to here. I remember shivering as I was moved. I had no idea what was happening. It is a shame I could not live out my life, but it is ok. I will come back when the time is right. To try again. One thing you learn "in death" is that "life" isn't the only thing that matters. It is so easy to forget. In those few moments, life felt like chaos. Earth feels like chaos now, so I will wait some time before coming again. It was not a person or a wild animal that ended my life. It was a force you have yet to discover. Sometimes I wonder why me, but then I let it go. It was just me. Easier that way. I am content and NOT still shivering.

Impression

My hands were shaking when I first tapped into him. He knows more than he is saying, but not giving more detailed info. He feels VERY peaceful. Very thoughtful. Not angry at all.

7-5-20

Aaron Hedges

Dying alone is scary. Especially when you don't know what happened. I was pulled right up from the ground. I didn't feel anyone or see anyone. I was just floating upward. Then I blacked out. Or at least I have no other memory until I passed to here. I remember shivering as I was moved. I had no idea what was happening. It is a shame I could not live out my life, but it is ok. I will come back when the time is right. To try again. One thing you learn "in death" is that "life" isn't the only thing that matters. It is so easy to forget. In those few moments, life felt like chaos. Earth feels like chaos now, so I will wait some time before coming again. It was not a person or a wild animal that ended my life. It was a force you have yet to discover. Sometimes I wonder why me, but then I let it go. It was just me. Easier that way. I am content and **NOT** still shivering.

Impression:

My hands were shaking when I first tapped into him. He knows more than he is saying, but not giving more detailed info. He feels VERY peaceful. Very thoughtful. Not angry at all.

7.5.20 Aaron Hedges

At first I felt a vibration. I wasn't sure what was wrong with me, I felt an urge to slow down. I guess to see what I was feeling. Was I going to throw up? Did I need some water? To be clear... I did feel something, just not someone grab me by the shoulder or hit me with something. It was subtle. It was gradual. Maybe if I wasn't in tune with my body I wouldn't have slowed down. But it doesn't matter now — except for you to think about. Yes — travel with others. But also do not be afraid. For you end up where you are meant to be. Even if you can't think of that in the moment of trauma. My body began vibrating at a different level. It was a completely foreign feeling for me. It jolted me. It literally paralyzed me. That's how I fell behind. Yes, I was terrified. But I was also mesmerized. I was enchanted and wanted to learn more. I stayed with them some time before I left my body. Though it didn't seem like a choice, it was. On a very deep level. Not a mental level, but something deep in my gut. It felt like the right thing at the right time. Pretty sure they "put" that feeling in me, but I own it and it is ok.

Impression

Not sad about life ending, trying to express something w/ the vibration... I got that when you practice diff. vibrations intentionally, you won't be apt to allow being taken over.

7-5-20

Aaron Hedges

At first I felt a vibration. I wasn't sure what was wrong with me. I felt an urge to slow down. I guess to see what I was feeling. Was I going to throw up? Did I need some water? To be clear...I did feel something, just not someone grabbing me by the shoulder or hitting me with something. It was subtle. It was gradual. Maybe if I wasn't in tune with my body I wouldn't have slowed down. But it doesn't matter now - except for you to think about. Yes - travel with others. But also do not be afraid. For you end up where you are meant to be. Even if you can't think of that in the moment of trauma. My body began vibrating at a different level. It was a completely foreign feeling to me. It jolted me. It literally paralyzed me. That's how I fell behind. Yes, I was terrified. But I was also mesmerized. I was enchanted and wanted to learn more. I stayed with them some time before I left my body. Though it didn't seem like a choice, it was. On a very deep level. Not a mental level, but something deep in my gut. It felt like the right thing at the right time. Pretty sure they "put" that feeling in me, but I own it and it is ok.

Impression:

Not sad about life ending, trying to express something with the vibration...I got that when you practice different vibrations intentionally, you won't be apt to allow being taken over.

7.5.20 Creature above Aaron

Four men go into the woods and start shooting animals. It is a game to them. They get their trophy and meat. Yet when one of them goes missing or dies— it causes a great panic. For a moment did any of those four think about the loss the were creating when taking the life of the animal? What about its family or pack? This is not a game we are playing. But you must see, sometimes it ~~too~~ looks like it. Ours is not a search for trophies, but a scientific inquiry. Much like hunters see it is their "right" to take a life, we see one simple/sole human as a tool for our understanding. You kill insects, plants, animals... you destroy your very land. Why do you put such unequal weight on a human life? Think about this. We also work to protect ourselves. We do that by learning about you. It ~~just~~ appears unusual and selfish to you. It sounds logical to us. See both sides. When you see us as un-harmful, we will not harm. When you see us as peaceful, we will show you peace. When you see us as a threat, we will attack. When you see us as intelligent, we will share what we know.
Aaron wanted to be with us. He was extremely curious. We did not take his life the way you think (probably). It was a mutual collaboration.

Impression
    Still not telling us everything, but showing us LOA is a thing of them too. They are afraid of our violence.

7-5-20

Creature above Aaron

Four men go into the woods and start shooting animals. It is a game to them. They get their trophy and meat. Yet when one of them goes missing or dies - it causes a great panic. For a moment did any of those four think about the loss they were creating when taking the life of the animal? What about its family or pack? This is not a game we are playing. But you must see, sometimes it looks like it. Ours is not a search for trophies, but a scientific inquiry. Much like hunters see it is their "right" to take a life, we see one simple/sole human as a tool for our understanding. You kill insects, plants, animals...you destroy your very land. Why do you put such unequal weight on a human life? Think about this. We also work to protect ourselves. We do that by learning about you. It appears unusual and selfish to you. It sounds logical to us. See both sides. When you see us as un-harmful, we will not harm you. When you see us as peaceful, we will show you peace. When you see us as a threat, we will attack. When you see us as intelligent, we will share what we know.

Aaron wanted to be with us. He was extremely curious. We didn't take his life the way you think (probably). It was a mutual collaboration.

Impression:
Still not telling us everything, but showing us Law Of Attraction is a thing with them too. They are afraid of our violence.

7.9.20   Aaron Hedges

I would like to tell you to never hold back. You live your life for a finite period of time. If you wait to do what makes you happy or gets you that fulfilled feeling, then you are not truly living life. You are floating through time. Don't know what you want and so are waiting around to figure it out? Well then... you are wasting a precious life. Yes, it sounds judgemental, but it is'n fact. You are given only so much time in this life. If you sit around watching TV and ignore your potential, you are wasting. Killing yourself in a way. Seize your day. Know what you are meant to do and learn each day. Take a priority for making an impression—on your own life. Yes, you must have down time, but you must also not waste time. When you accept the value of your time, you will grow ever faster, put together the bits you need to make sense of why you are here in the first place. Don't over-work yourself, but also don't be lazy. Use your time wisely, for it could vanish before you expect, before you know. Seize your day.

Impression:

He does not have regrets about his last days — he was happy and loved his life. Encourages us to do the same. He died happy.

7-9-20

Aaron Hedges

I would like to tell you to never hold back. You live your life for a finite period of time. If you wait to do what makes you happy or gets you to that fulfilled feeling, then you are not truly living life. You are floating through time. Don't know what you want and so are waiting around to figure it out? Well then...you are <u>wasting</u> a precious life. Yes, it sounds judgemental, but it is a fact. You are given only so much time in this life. If you sit around watching TV and ignore your potential, you are wasting, killing yourself in a way. Seize your day. Know what you are meant to do and learn each day. Take a priority for making an impression - on your own life. Yes, you must have down time, but you must also not waste time. When you accept the value of your time, you will grow even faster, put together the bits you need to make sense of why you are here in the first place. Don't overwork yourself, but also don't be lazy. Use your time wisely, for it could vanish before you expect, before you know. Seize your day.

Impression:

He doesn't have regrets about his last days - he was happy and loved his life. Encourages us to do the same. He died happy.

7.9.20 Entity of Aaron Hedges

You have to know when it is the time for action and when it is time to wait. You might have in your mind that you want to do something, so you get distracted from the "right" timing and just move - more - move. When you can't listen to the right timing then you fail to accomplish what you want. So this is a lesson. What can you do while you (WAITS) find the right time? Writing seems hard sometimes, but it is very necessary. You can easily spoil the entire plan by moving in the wrong time. How can you develop the patience necessary to know when is the right time? Once you can see that it is not all about you, but about the collective good, then timing becomes abundantly clear. And when timing is right, projects get completed more easily, with with more ease, and more proficiently. Meaning — it all goes well. So take your time, set out right... wait if necessary so you can accomplish what you need in the right way.

Impression

They are not randomly taking people — experiments are not at random. There is no rush. Timing is everything

7-9-20

Entity of Aaron Hedges

You have to know when it is time for action and when it is time to wait. You might have in your mind that you want to do something, so you get distracted from the "right" timing and just move - move - move. When you can't listen to the right timing, often you fail to accomplish what you want. So this is a lesson. What can you do while you wait to find the right time? Waiting seems hard sometimes, but it is very necessary. You can easily spoil the entire plan by moving in the wrong time. How can you develop the patience necessary to know when is the right time? Once you can see that it is not all about you, but about the collective good, then timing becomes abundantly clear. And when timing is right, projects get completed more easily, with more ease, and more proficiently! Meaning - it all goes well. So take your time, set out right...wait if necessary so you can accomplish what you need in the right way.

Impression:

They are not randomly taking people - experiments are not at random. There is no rush. Timing is everything.

7-14-20 Aaron's guy

You already know this, but will outline it
again - magnets play a major factor in
how we operate. You must study more about
magnetism if you want to understand about
non human interactions. It is the simultaneous
spinning of various magnets that allow us
to move in ways you don't comprehend.
Magnetism also works with thoughts. We leave
this to you to investigate for now. It is how
you feel us. Think of the vibration of
magnetism. This is how we are connected.

Impression
     wants you to think or research this ideas
will be back to explain more.

7-14-20

Aaron's guy

You already know this, but will outline it again - magnets play a major factor in how we operate. You must study more about magnetism if you want to understand about non human interactions. It is the simultaneous spinning of various magnets that allow us to move in ways you don't comprehend. Magnetism also works with thoughts. We leave this to you to investigate for now. It is how you feel us. Think of the vibration of magnetism. This is how we are connected.

Impression:

Wants you to think or research this idea and will be back to explain more.

7-18-20   Aaron Entity

Rolling road blocks and tunnel vision. You might not know where you are or where you are going but you are there. Not just exactly where you "should" be, but along the way. Do not be disheartened with the size of the hills and do not get blocked by the tunnel vision. Know there is always something at the end of the road. There is always a way out. Sooner or later you get there. When you think you need to be there now is when the hill gets deeper, or the tunnel feels darker. The trick is to ease up. Those who push too hard have the most resistance. Find the steady step. Find the ease is floating. For truly it is a matter of the movement. How do we get from here to there undetected. Certainly you want to know our method, but some things are better left Unknown. Not that you can't know the truth, but it is better if it can find you. Notice the absence of objects on the hills and in the tunnel. There is nothing there more than space. And of course your mind. Clear your mind even further. Let it go more. There you will see you are right where you are meant to be.

Impression
It feels like the hills & tunnel are a specific place. Maybe a place you've been before?

7-18-20

Aaron Entity

Rolling road blocks and tunnel vision. You might not know where you are or where you are going but you are there. Not just exactly where you "should" be, but along the way. Do not be disheartened with the size of the hills and do not get blocked by the tunnel vision. Know there is always something at the end of the road. There is always a way out. Sooner or later you get there. When you think you need to be there now is when the hill gets deeper, or the tunnel feels darker. The trick is to ease up. Those who push too hard have the most resistance. Find the steady step. Find the ease in floating. For truly it is a matter of the movement. How do we get from here to there undetected? Certainly you want to know our method, but some things are better left unknown. Not that you can't know the truth, but it is better if it can find you. Notice the absence of objects on the hills and in the tunnel. There is nothing there more than space. And of course your mind. Clear your mind even further. Let it go more. There you will see you are right where you are meant to be.

Impression:
It feels like the hills and the tunnel are a specific place. Maybe a place you've been before?

8.28.20   Aaron

Check the recurrent language. Sometimes words come into your day and you don't really pay attention. You are focused more on the meaning than the word. If you can step back and see each word — see which one comes up multiple times. This is the message you are meant to hear. Of course you still must figure out the "meaning" of the word in your life. BUT if you are "searching" and find it hard to know, pay attention to the individual words. You might understand that when you focus so much, so intently on what you are reading and hearing that you realize you are TRULY living mindfully. Be present — ALL THE TIME. Hear/See the words that are important to you right now. See them open up your mind for connection. These / This word(s) is NOT by chance — it is to open your connection so you can use the knowledge to BETTER yourself. Listen. Completely. What words do you hear repeated?

Impression
This is MORE than a mindfulness practice. It is about seeing where and how you are connected in the universe. Words have vibration AND meaning. PAY ATTENTION.

8-28-20

Aaron

Check the recurrent language. Sometimes words come into your day and you don't really pay attention. You are focused more on the meaning than the word. If you can step back and see each word - see which one comes up multiple times. This is the message you are meant to hear. Of course you still must figure out the "meaning" of the word in your life. BUT if you are "searching" and find it hard to know, pay attention to the individual words. You might understand that when you focus so much, so intently on what you are reading and hearing that you realize you are TRULY living mindfully. Be present - ALL THE TIME. Hear/See the words that are important to you right now. See them open up your mind for connection. These/ This word(s) is NOT by chance - it is to open your connection so you can use the knowledge to BETTER yourself. Listen. Completely. What words do you hear repeated?

Impression:

This is MORE than a mindfulness practice. It is about seeing where and how you are connected in the universe. Words have vibration AND meaning. PAY ATTENTION.

10-9-20   Aaron

Like the leaves drip down to the ground in fall, so too can you leave your mark - in sweat, tears, blood, energy, footprints on the land below you. Each impression lasts for its specific amount of time before it is absorbed into the earth. Then you think it is never to be seen or known again. This is only partially true. All that drips or falls down is energy, and that energy is absorbed by the ground, transforming the very earth on which we live. So think about that as you leave your traces behind. Will you knowingly leave your negative impact? Will you try to raise the vibration of the earth? When you ground yourself, will you GIVE or will you TAKE the earths energy? Know you have an impact. Know you are completely connected. It isn't just the trash you leave... it is also your tears, your love, your beauty. Maybe try to leave more positive elements — see how you can exert less negative from your being. That starts with you having more happiness, joy, light within you to start. Then you can't help but trickle this out INto the world. Remember, you are ONE with the earth, even if you think you are separate.

Impression
Be more perceptile of your natural surroundings. Think about what you can give not always what you get. It is a dual relationship. This talks about energy you give earth — think also what energy you are receiving.

10-9-20

Aaron

Like the leaves drip down to the ground in the fall, so too can you leave your mark - in sweat, tears, blood, energy, footprints on the land below you. Each impression lasts for its specific amount of time before it is absorbed into the earth. Then you think it is never to be seen or known again. This is only partially true. All that drips or falls down is energy, and that energy is absorbed by the ground, transforming the very earth on which we live. So think about that as you leave your traces behind. Will you knowingly leave your negative impact? Will you try to raise the vibration of the earth? When you ground yourself, will you GIVE or will you Take the earth's energy? Know you have an impact. Know you are completely connected. It isn't just the trash you leave...it is also your tears, your love, your beauty. Maybe try to leave more positive elements - see how you can exert less negative from your being. That starts with you having more happiness, joy, light within you to start. Then you can't help but trickle this out IN to the world. Remember, you are ONE with the earth, even if you think you are separate.

Impression:
Be more perceptive of your natural surroundings. Think about what you can give, not always what you get. It is a dual relationship. This talks about energy you give earth - think also what energy you are receiving.

11.1.20   Aaron Hedges

Were you ever so absorbed in what you were doing that you hurt yourself? Imagine bouncing along, wandering on a trail, enjoying all that nature gives us, and you fall flat on your face. Makes you wonder, right? In that moment you think you are full of gratitude and joyous, you fall down, stumble, as if you weren't paying attention. As if the opposite should have happened. It is a fine line — don't get too distracted while you are in the midst of joy. You have to still stay here on the ground! It is sort of a bummer, though actually. You can't just get blissed out while you are engaged in a movement activity or you could be in personal danger. Go ahead and enjoy what you can, but also keep your wits about you. Your personal safety is at stake. I'm not saying this to startle you or make you paranoid. Just to help keep you aware of the reality. Could be worse than a sprained ankle. So please watch your absorption. You can thank me later.

Impression
It feels like this is what happened to him. He wasn't paying attention and something tragic happened. This is his way of taking responsibility for his absent mindedness. No blame. Keep your head up.

11-1-20

Aaron

Were you ever so absorbed in what you were doing that you hurt yourself? Imagine bouncing along, wandering on a trail, enjoying all that nature gives us, and you fall flat on your face. Makes you wonder, right? In that moment you think you are full of gratitude and joyous, you fall down, stumble, as if you weren't paying attention. As if the opposite should have happened. It is a fine line - don't get too distracted while you are in the midst of joy. You have to still stay here on the ground. It is sort of a bummer, though actually, you can't just get blissed out while you are engaged in a movement activity or you could be in personal danger. Go ahead and enjoy what you can, but also keep your wits about you. Your personal safety is at stake. I'm not saying this to startle you or make you paranoid. Just to help keep you aware of the reality. Could be worse than a sprained ankle. So please watch your absorption. You can thank me later.

Impression:

It feels like this is what happened to him. He wasn't paying attention and something tragic happened. This is his way of taking responsibility for his absent mindedness. No blame. Keep your head up.

11.11.20 Aaron

There is a flame of knowledge in every person. This fire can be made bigger or smaller depending on the amount of attention somebody puts on it. Dedicate yourself to learning something new, the flame grows brighter, stronger. Same can be said in the opposite way. Often something outside of yourself can give you an instant knowledge. Most people do not understand this, and will discount something "known" that they don't remember reading or hearing. It is seen as unverifiable, and thus not truly known.

I saw a disc of light and I knew in an instant so many things I previously didn't know. When you are hit with this kind of (vast) information, the flame within grows so large, almost instantly, that you have a surge inside you — it feels like a shock of love. Near euphoria. In that instant nothing else matters. Like when you are touched by god. Like a warm hand is covering your heart. It is warm and comforting and feels like a rare blessing. I think I was so in shock that day that my heart stopped. But it didn't matter at all, because nothing mattered. I felt true, pure love. And it was light.

Be open along your life for these flashes. See them in pieces so you don't receive a shock that ends your life too soon.

Impression

Be aware of what you are exposed to daily. Too often we miss so much of what happens in our lives. We are distracted, not paying attention, or just don't care. Intuitive knowledge is all around — open your eyes and heart) to see it.

11-11-20

Aaron

There is a flame of knowledge in every person. This fire can be made bigger or smaller depending on the amount of attention somebody puts on it. Dedicate yourself to learning something new, the flame grows brighter, stronger. Same can be said in the opposite way. Often something outside of yourself can give you an instant knowledge. Most people do not understand this, and will discount something "known" that they don't remember reading or hearing. It is seen as unverifiable, and thus not truly known. I saw a disc of light and I knew in an instant so many things I previously didn't know. When you are hit with this kind of (vast) information, the flame within grows so large, almost instantly, that you have a surge inside you - it feels like a shock of love. Near euphoria. In that instant nothing else matters, like when you are touched by god. Like a warm hand is covering your heart. It is warm and comforting and feels like a rare blessing. I think I was so in shock that day that my heart stopped. But it didn't matter at all, because nothing mattered. I felt true, pure love. And it was light. Be open along your life for those flashes. See them in pieces so you don't receive a shock that ends your life too soon.

Impression:

Be aware of what you are exposed to daily. Too often we miss so much of what happens in our lives. We are distracted, not paying attention, or just don't care. Intuitive knowledge is all around - open your eyes (and heart) to see it.

1·23·21   Aaron

Always looking behind me – also to the right and left – even up ahead. Never can be too sure of your safety. That's what you realize, when you see how short life can be. You just don't know what might happen. I'm not recommending this way of life to anyone, because you end up feeling paranoid and distrustful. Not every life is so fragile. Meaning cut short. Even now, I am watching in all directions – trying to sense that which is around me that is unsensible. It helps me sometimes to "hug" a tree – to clutch on for dear life. Maybe this is what it is like in a tsunami. Find a tree, hold on, try to climb taller/higher as if there is safety the higher you go – and as if the tree is "untouchable". Imagine many people hanging on to trees for dear life. How hard would you grasp? Tight enough to fight for your life? Or are you inclined to give up, to feel defeated? Neither is wrong. It is not a question. Pay attention, but not so much that you loose your connection to the here and now.

Impression

I see him looking back at life and wishing he would have held onto a tree.

1-23-21

Aaron

Always looking behind me - also to the right and left - even up ahead. Never can be too sure of your safety. That's what you realize, when you see how short life can be. You just don't know what might happen. I'm not recommending this way of life to anyone, because you end up feeling paranoid and distrustful. Not every life is so fragile. Meaning cut short. Even now, I am watching in all directions - trying to sense that which is around me that is unsensible. It helps me sometimes to "hug" a tree - to clutch on for dear life. Maybe this is what it is like in a tsunami. Find a tree, hold on, try to climb taller/ higher as if there is safety the higher you go - and as if the tree is "untouchable." Imagine many people hanging on to trees for dear life. How hard would you grasp? Tight enough to fight for your life? Or are you inclined to give up, to feel defeated? Neither is wrong. It is just a question. Pay attention, but not so much that you lose your connection to the here and now.

Impression:
I see him looking back at life and wishing he would have held onto a tree.

ABOUT THE AUTHOR

Amelia Hathow is a recently retired elementary school teacher, who after three years studying and practicing her mediumship abilities, she wrote her first book from channeled messages she received. Her first book considers the Rapture through the story of a hunter who was killed on a hunting trip.